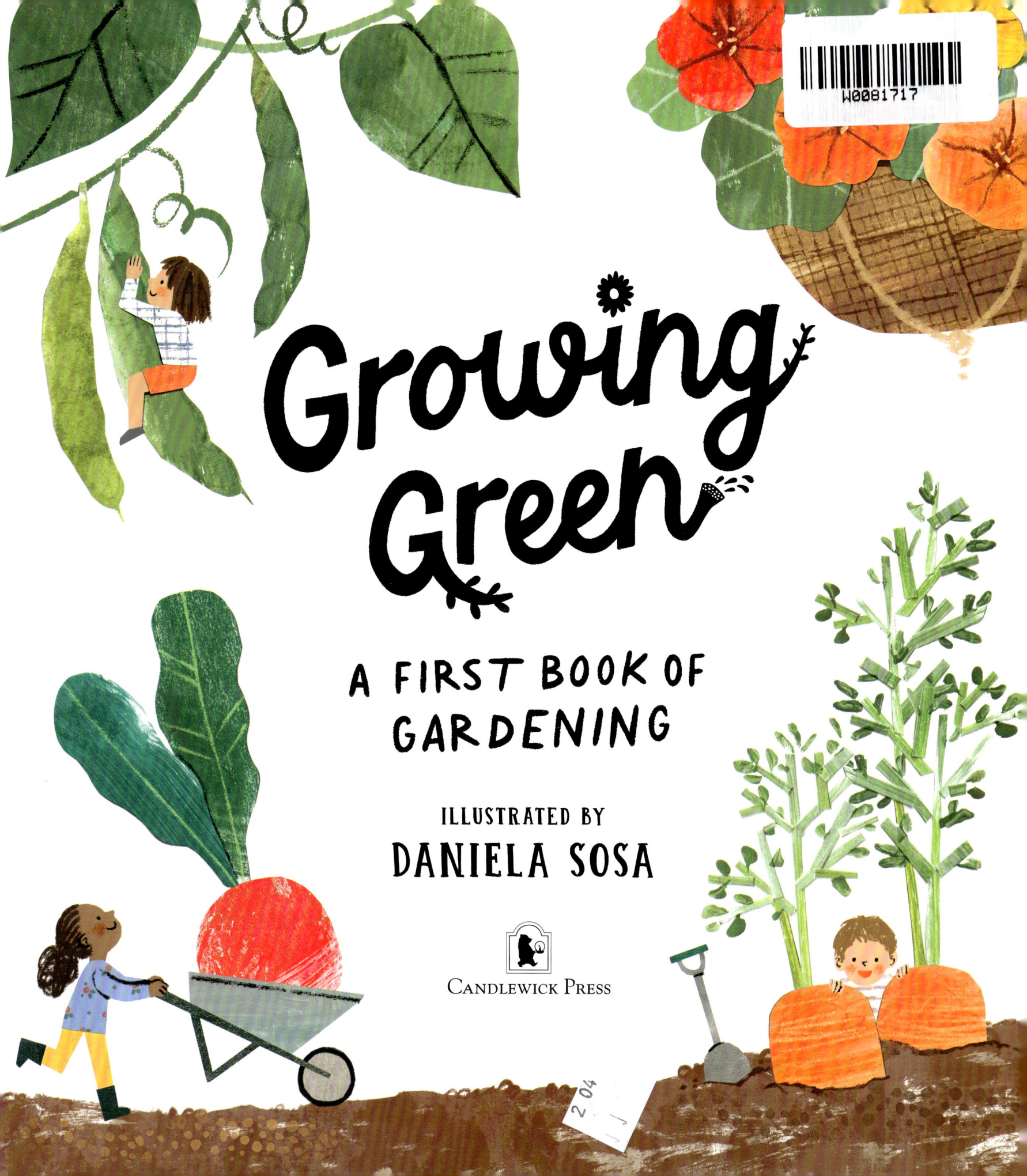

Growing Green

A FIRST BOOK OF GARDENING

ILLUSTRATED BY

DANIELA SOSA

CANDLEWICK PRESS

CONTENTS

GETTING STARTED

Gardening is great! It's an amazing (often) outdoor activity where you can really get your hands dirty! Planting a seed, caring for it, and watching it grow is easy and fun—and there's nothing more delicious than a juicy, ripe strawberry that you've grown yourself.

You'll need some basic tools: compost (make sure it's peat-free to preserve natural habitats), a trowel and a small garden fork, a watering can, labels and garden twine—and, of course, seeds! You may want to wear gardening gloves, especially if you need to do any weeding. You don't have to buy everything, though. Raid your recycling: egg cartons make great trays for seedlings, and yogurt cups can be used instead of plant pots (remember to make drainage holes). If you ask an adult to pierce some holes in the lid of a plastic juice bottle, you'll have a homemade watering can, and you can make your own compost from kitchen scraps and garden waste.

You don't need a lot of space—you don't even need a garden. There are projects in this book that you can do on your kitchen counter and lots more that can be grown on windowsills and in pots. It's amazing how much you can grow on a balcony, and if you have access to a community garden plot, the sky's the limit.

So why grow your own fruit and vegetables? Well, being self-sufficient is good for the planet. It creates less plastic waste than buying veggies at the store, it reduces your carbon footprint, and best of all, it means you get to choose what you want to grow and eat.

Look after your plants well. Water them when the soil around the base begins to feel dry. When you need to move seedlings to a bigger pot, handle them with care. If you are planting seedlings outdoors, harden them up by taking them outside during the day for a few days to get them used to a different climate.

Whatever you choose to grow, have fun and enjoy growing green!

YOU WILL NEED:

- An old pair of rain boots
- Screwdriver/drill/scissors
- Stones/gravel
- Compost
- 4 strawberry plants
- Trowel
- Plant food

STRAWBERRIES IN RAIN BOOTS

Strawberries are sweet, delicious, and easy to grow! Each plant can give you a good crop of fruit for three to four years. Plant in early May and you should see a healthy harvest from June and July onward.

SEASON

HARVEST

ENVIRONMENT

Spring, summer & autumn

4–6 weeks

Outdoors

HOW TO GROW:

1 Remove the insoles from the rain boots and ask an adult to pierce holes in the bottom of each boot using a screwdriver or a drill.

2 Create a shallow layer of stones or gravel inside each boot to help with drainage, then fill both boots nearly to the top with compost.

3 Get an adult to make a slit halfway up one side of each boot.

4 Now, plant a seedling in the top of each boot. The base of the plant, where the stalks start, should be at the same level as the soil.

6 Make sure that your rain boots are in a sunny spot and water them every day. Feed them once a week with plant food.

5 Get your hands dirty and scoop out enough soil from the side pockets to plant another strawberry in each.

7 When you see fruit, you may want to cover your plants with a bit of netting to keep the birds from snacking!

8 Check your plants every day and harvest them when your strawberries look big, juicy, and red-ripe. Eat them right away!

CHERRY TOMATOES IN HANGING BASKETS

If you don't have much space, a great way to grow tomatoes is in a hanging basket. You can grow them from seed or buy plants from your local garden center in late spring/early summer.

YOU WILL NEED:

- A hanging basket
- A liner (a circle cut from an old compost bag is ideal)
- Compost
- Cherry tomato plants (make sure you use a "tumbling" variety)
- Plant food

SEASON	HARVEST	ENVIRONMENT
Spring & summer	6-12 weeks	Outdoors

PLANT FOOD

HOW TO GROW:

1 Line your basket with recycled plastic and make 5 or 6 holes in the bottom for drainage. You may need an adult to help you with this. Then fill the basket about $^2/_3$ of the way up with compost.

2 Arrange your plants inside. There should be space for 2–4 plants. Place them near the outside edge of the basket so that they will be able to trail down the sides.

4 Gently tap down the compost, water the plants, and hang your basket in a sunny spot.

3 Make sure that the base of each plant is about level with the top of the basket, then fill with compost.

5 Water regularly and feed with plant food every 2 weeks once they start to flower.

6 Within a few weeks, you will begin to see tomatoes. Check for ripe fruit every few days and gently pull them off the plant.

DID YOU KNOW?

Tomato plants were first grown for food by the Aztecs in the Americas. Now, every year in August, 20,000 people gather in the Spanish town of Buñol for an epic tomato-throwing festival. More than 110 tons/100 metric tons of overripe tomatoes are thrown in the streets!

GREEN BEANS

Green beans are really easy to grow. There are two main types of green beans: bush beans (which grow in a compact space) and pole beans (they grow in climbing vines). You can grow either in your garden! Seeds can be planted indoors in April and transplanted outside in May or sown straight into the ground anytime after the last spring frost.

YOU WILL NEED:

- Small pots
- Compost
- Seeds (make sure you know if it is a bush or pole bean)
- Labels and a pen
- Large pots (or a vegetable patch)
- A trowel
- Garden stakes and string

SEASON	HARVEST	ENVIRONMENT
Spring & summer	2 months	Indoors & outdoors

HOW TO GROW:

BEANS

1 Fill small (3-inch/8 cm diameter) pots with compost. Using your finger, poke a hole in the center about 1 inch/2.5 cm deep.

2 Drop one bean seed into each hole, cover with soil, and water well.

3 Put a label in each pot so you don't forget what you've planted, and move them to a sunny windowsill. Water them a little each day so they don't dry out.

5 Choose where to plant them—you can transfer them to a large pot or straight into the soil. Use your trowel to dig a hole the same size as your small pot.

4 Seeds will germinate in about a week, and you should see green shoots emerge. After 3 weeks, your seedlings should be ready to plant outside.

6 Carefully tap out the seedling and place in the hole. Fill in any space around it with soil or compost.

7 If you have planted a pole bean variety, you will need to support the plants by creating a "bean cage" with garden stakes (or sticks) and string. Carefully wrap the plants around it.

8 Pick your beans as soon as the pods are swollen and ready to harvest. More beans should grow if you harvest them regularly.

NEW POTATOES

Digging your own new potatoes out of the ground makes them much, much tastier than store-bought spuds. They're fun to grow in either a vegetable patch or a large pot. You can also get special grow bags if you don't have much space in your garden.

YOU WILL NEED:

- Seed potatoes
- Old egg cartons
- A trowel
- A vegetable patch (or a large pot or grow bag)
- Labels and a pen
- A small garden fork
- Compost

SEASON	HARVEST	ENVIRONMENT
Spring & summer	10–12 weeks	Outdoors

HOW TO GROW:

1 In early February, buy some seed potatoes. Six will give you plenty of potatoes! Make sure you buy "early" potatoes to grow small, new potatoes.

2 With the "eyes" (little buds of growth) at the top, put one seed potato in each pocket of the egg carton. Leave on a sunny windowsill until they start to sprout. This is known as "chitting."

3 Toward the end of March, the soil should be warm enough to plant your chitted potatoes outside.

6 The potato plants will grow quickly, and you should begin to see shoots after about 2–4 weeks.

5 Label them and give them a really good watering, especially as the weather gets warmer. The potatoes will need around 1–2 inches/2.5–5 cm of water each week.

4 If planting them in a container, make sure that it can drain easily. Fill it with compost to about 1 inch/2.5 cm from the top, then plant your chits 4–6 inches/10–15 cm deep.

7 When the shoots are 4 inches/10 cm above ground level, you need to mound the soil up around the stalks. This is called "hilling," and it helps you get a really good crop.

8 In June and July, the plants will begin to flower. When they have finished flowering, they should be ready to harvest.

9 To harvest, use a garden fork to dig under the plant and lever up the crop. If you're using containers, you can just turn them upside down and help yourself!

CARROTS

Carrots can be grown for a good part of the year, from March to July. They are packed full of nutrients and can be found in many colors—even purple and white!

SEASON	HARVEST	ENVIRONMENT
Spring, summer & autumn	3–4 months	Outdoors

YOU WILL NEED:

- A vegetable patch or a large pot
- Compost
- A small garden fork
- A rake
- Carrot seeds

HOW TO GROW:

1 If you are growing the carrots straight into your garden, you will need to dig up the ground to break up the soil and make sure that it is weed-free. You may want to get an adult to help you with this! If you're using big pots, fill the pots nearly to the top with compost.

2 Rake over the surface of the soil (or compost) and drag your finger through the soil to make a line (½ inch/1 cm deep). If you are growing more than one row, make sure that the rows are 1 foot/30 cm apart.

3 Sow the seeds into each row, ¼ inch/.5 cm deep, 2–3 inches/5–8 cm apart, then cover gently, and water. Make sure to keep the soil moist with frequent, shallow waterings.

DID YOU KNOW?
Carrots are full of beta-carotene—this gives them their orange color and turns into vitamin A in your body, which is very good for your eyesight.

4 When the seeds start to sprout, in about 2–3 weeks, thin them out so that they are 2–3 inches/5–8 cm apart.

5 If the tops of the carrots become visible above the ground, just cover them up with more soil or compost. Make sure to keep your carrots weed-free.

6 When the tops of the carrots measure about ½ inch/1 cm across, it's time to dig them up. Simply grab the base of the stalks and pull! If you have a huge crop, dig them up in stages, so you can stagger your harvest over time.

SWEET CORN

Super-sweet corn on the cob tastes even more delicious when it's eaten fresh from your garden. Sown in April or May, it is best started indoors then planted out into large containers or straight into the ground, 2–3 weeks after the last frost. It likes a sunny but sheltered spot, so next to a wall would be a good place. It doesn't like to have its roots disturbed so is best sown in a cardboard tube, which can then be planted straight into the ground.

YOU WILL NEED:

- Toilet paper tubes
- Compost
- Sweet corn seeds
- Labels and a pen
- A vegetable patch or a large pot
- A trowel

SEASON	HARVEST	ENVIRONMENT
Spring, summer & autumn	2-4 months	Indoors & outdoors

DID YOU KNOW?

There are about 800 kernels on each ear of corn!

HOW TO GROW:

1 Fill your toilet paper rolls nearly to the top with compost, water lightly, and poke two holes (1½ inches/4 cm deep) in each with your finger.

2 Pop a seed in each hole, cover them over with compost, and water gently. Label the tubes and leave them on a sunny windowsill.

3 When the seeds have germinated—usually after about 10 days—remove the weaker of the two seedlings.

5 Arrange your containers in a cluster rather than a line so that the plants will be successfully pollinated. Water once a week.

4 When all danger of frost has passed, and your seedlings look strong enough to transplant, plant them outside in large pots or straight into the ground. If you are planting into a vegetable patch, you will need to keep them 12–18 inches/30–45 cm apart.

6 After they have flowered, the cobs will begin to grow inside protective leaves. You may need to water them more often at this stage.

7 When the "silks" at the top of the cobs begin to turn dark brown, your corn will be ready to harvest. Gently peel back the leaves and check that the kernels are bright yellow and plump.

8 To harvest, simply twist the cobs off the main stalk, pulling sharply.

PUMPKINS

To harvest your pumpkin crop by Halloween, plant seeds from late May if you live in the northern US and from early July if you are in the southern US. Pumpkins can take up a lot of space, so you may need to plant these straight into the ground—though there are mini varieties available if you only have room for pots.

YOU WILL NEED:

- Pumpkin seeds
- Small pots or yogurt cups with holes in the bottom
- Compost
- Labels and a pen
- A trowel
- Plant food

SEASON	HARVEST	ENVIRONMENT
Summer & autumn	3–4 months	Outdoors

DID YOU KNOW?
The largest-ever pumpkin was grown in Italy in 2021. It weighed more than 2,702 pounds/1,226 kg, which is about the same size as a small car!

HOW TO GROW:

1 Soak your seeds overnight before you plant them—it will help them germinate.

2 Fill your pots nearly to the top with compost, water lightly, and make a hole (1 inch/2.5 cm deep) in each with your finger.

3 Pop a seed in each hole, making sure that it points up rather than lying on its flat side, and cover with compost.

7 Place it gently in the hole and then fill in any gaps around your plant with more compost. Water gently.

6 Dig a hole in your vegetable patch that is slightly bigger than your pot, and put some more compost in the bottom. Carefully tip the seedling out, protecting the root growth.

5 Water them every couple of days, and when they are about 4-6 inches/10-15 cm tall, they should be ready to transplant into the garden. Place in rows, with at least 18 inches/46 cm between plants.

4 Label your pots and put them on a warm, sunny windowsill (or in a greenhouse if you have access to one).

8 You'll need to keep your pumpkins well watered throughout the summer and protect your plants from pests.

9 When the pumpkins start to grow, feed your plant with plant food every 2 weeks. You may want to put a piece of cardboard or an old piece of wood underneath the pumpkins to prevent them from getting soggy and rotting.

10 The pumpkins will be ready to harvest when they are a deep, solid color and the stems begin to crack. After you've cut them from the plant, leave them in the sun for a week so that their skins harden.

AVOCADO PITS

These can be grown all year round on a sunny windowsill in your home. They make lovely houseplants, but be aware that if you want to grow your own avocados to eat, it will take at least five years!

YOU WILL NEED:

- An avocado seed (pit)
- 3 toothpicks
- A clean jam jar
- A medium-size pot
- Compost
- Plant food

HOW TO GROW:

1 The next time you're eating an avocado, ask an adult to carefully remove the seed with a knife. Wash it and leave to dry for 2–3 days.

2 Holding the round end down, pierce the pit around the middle with the 3 toothpicks, spacing them equally, then balance it across the top of the jar.

10 Pat the soil down to make sure that the seed is stable, then take out the toothpicks. Water it sparingly and feed it once a week with plant food.

9 Place it gently in the pot and, still holding the stem, add more soil until it reaches about a third of the way up the seed.

DID YOU KNOW?

Avocados are incredibly high in potassium, which helps keep your heart healthy.

3 Add enough water to reach halfway up the pit.

4 Put the jar on a warm, sunny windowsill and change the water every 5 days to stop any algae from growing.

5 After about 4–6 weeks, you should see some root growth developing.

8 Half-fill a 6–8 inch/15–20 cm wide plant pot with soil or compost. Carefully lift the seed out of the jam jar, picking it up by the stem so that the pit itself doesn't split.

7 As long as the leaves look healthy, you can keep it in the jam jar, but as soon as the leaves start to turn yellow or dry out, you need to transplant it to a plant pot.

6 After 7–8 weeks, you should see a shoot coming out of the top and the seed will split in half. By 10 weeks, you should have some leaves growing.

CELERY BOTTOMS

This is one of the easiest things that you can grow from kitchen scraps, and it can be grown on any windowsill. You can grow it outdoors in spring or autumn and anytime of the year indoors.

YOU WILL NEED:

- The bottom of a head of celery
- A small bowl
- Water
- A medium pot
- Compost

DID YOU KNOW?

Celery is a great source of antioxidants and has been used to treat toothaches, sleeplessness, and anxiety. Winners of athletic events in ancient Greece would be presented with a bunch of celery, just like modern-day winners are given flowers!

SEASON	HARVEST	ENVIRONMENT
All year round	About 5 months	Indoors

HOW TO GROW:

 1 The next time anyone is cooking with celery in your house, ask an adult to cut the bottom off, leaving 2–3 inches/5–8 cm of the stalks intact.

 2 Fill a small bowl with 1 inch/ 2.5 cm of water, then take 3 or 4 of the outer stems off the celery bottom and place it in the bowl.

 3 Place the bowl on a sunny windowsill and change the water every 2–3 days to keep it fresh.

 6 When you see the roots (there may not be many), you can transfer it into a medium pot (about 8 inches/20 cm across). Fill the pot with compost, then water it really well until it is soggy.

5 After about 2 weeks, roots should begin to form—usually at the sides.

 4 After about 6 days, you should be able to see growth in the center of the celery bottom.

 7 Put the celery bottom on the top of the compost and add in another 1 inch/2.5 cm of compost around it. Pat it down firmly to secure the base.

 8 Wait until your new plant reaches full size, then harvest the stalks.

RADISHES

These tasty round roots add color and crunch to your lunch. They grow quickly and can be sown straight into the ground in both the spring and the fall.

SEASON	HARVEST	ENVIRONMENT
All year round	4–8 weeks	Indoors & outdoors

HOW TO GROW:

1 Make sure that your patch of earth or pot is completely weed-free before you plant by digging out any weeds with a trowel.

2 Use a rake or fork to break up any large lumps of soil until you have a smooth, crumbly surface to plant in.

3 Draw a line in the soil with your trowel, making a groove about ½ inch/1 cm deep.

6 After 4–6 weeks, you will begin to see radishes that are ready for eating. Pick them when they measure approximately 1 inch/2.5 cm across, before they grow too big and peppery.

5 Water the soil, and as the seedlings grow, thin them out by removing the weaker ones. Leave 1-inch/2.5 cm spaces between the remaining plants so that they have enough room to grow.

4 Sprinkle the radish seeds thinly along the groove and cover with soil. (If you are sowing more than one row, make sure that the rows are 6 inches/15 cm apart.)

24

CRESSHEADS

Cress can be grown indoors all year round. Making "cressheads" is quick, easy, and lots of fun!

YOU WILL NEED:

- 6 empty eggshells
- An egg carton
- Cotton balls
- Cress seeds
- Markers

SEASON	HARVEST	ENVIRONMENT
All year round	5–7 days	Indoors

1 Next time you use some eggs, carefully clean out the shells really well and save them up in an old egg carton, until you have a set of six.

2 Place a cotton ball inside each of the empty shells, and sprinkle a thin layer of cress seeds evenly across it.

4 Store them in a warm, sunny place. Keep the cotton ball moist, and your cress should begin to grow.

3 Draw faces on each of the eggs. You can turn them into whatever you like—let your imagination run wild! When you're done, carefully water inside each eggshell.

5 After about 7 days, you should have lots of lovely hair on your egg-heads.

6 Give them a trim and enjoy the cress in a tasty sandwich.

25

TIN CAN HERB GARDEN

Growing herbs on a kitchen windowsill will help you cook with flavor. Most herbs are easy to grow, but basil, mint, parsley, and cilantro all sprout particularly fast once sown.

SEASON	HARVEST	ENVIRONMENT
All year round	4–6 weeks	Indoors

HOW TO GROW:

1 Remove the labels and get an adult to completely remove the lids of your cans, making sure that there are no sharp edges.

2 Ask them to use the hammer and nail to punch a few drainage holes into the bottom of the cans.

3 Wash the cans carefully and paint the outsides with acrylic paints, then leave to dry. You can make them as decorative as you like.

10 For a continuous supply of herbs, you can add a few more seeds to the cans as you harvest.

9 After about 4–6 weeks, you should be able to start harvesting your herbs.

8 Continue watering whenever the compost begins to feel dry, and after about a week, you should begin to see your seeds sprouting.

BASIL

4 You can use a marker to write what type of herb you are going to grow in each pot, or use plant labels.

5 Fill the cans with compost until it reaches about ½ inch/1 cm from the top.

6 Choosing one type of herb for each can, sprinkle a few seeds evenly over the top of the compost.

7 Add a little more compost to cover up the seeds, then water them and set the cans down on an old plate or tray so that your windowsill doesn't get wet!

ENDLESS LEAFY GREENS

Leafy greens can be grown in a shallow pot on a sunny windowsill or balcony, in grow bags, or even straight into the ground in summer. Choose plants that have individual leaves (such as arugula or chard) and you can sow when you harvest for a continuous supply. If you are planting outside, make sure to research the best time of year to sow each type of seed.

SEASON	HARVEST	ENVIRONMENT
All year round	3–6 weeks	Indoors & outdoors

HOW TO GROW:

1 Fill your container nearly to the top with compost.

2 Rake over the surface so that it is even, then use your finger to draw straight lines in the soil (½ inch/1 cm deep and 4–6 inches/10–15 cm apart).

3 Water well, then lightly sprinkle the seeds into the grooves, spacing them about ½ inch/1 cm apart.

6 Throughout the growing season, add more seeds to the rows for more crops to harvest.

5 When the leaves are the right size to eat, cut them close to ground level. Be careful not to cut the heart of the plant, though, so that more leaves can grow.

4 Cover very lightly with compost or soil, and water regularly.

NASTURTIUMS

Nasturtiums are bright and colorful flowers with edible petals, leaves, and seeds. They're easy to grow and don't mind bad weather. Seeds can be planted outside in the spring, after all chance of frost has passed. There are three types of nasturtium (bush, trailing, and climbing), so make sure you select the right type for your space.

YOU WILL NEED:

- Nasturtium seeds
- A large pot (12-inch/30 cm diameter)
- Soil or compost

HOW TO GROW:

SEASON	HARVEST	ENVIRONMENT
Spring & summer	6-9 weeks	Indoors & outdoors

1 Fill a large plant pot with soil. It doesn't need to be expensive compost as nasturtiums will grow in just about anything.

2 Poke holes with your finger (about 1 inch/2.5 cm deep and 4 inches/ 10 cm apart).

3 Drop a seed into each hole, then cover it lightly with soil. Water well.

6 Harvest the flowers, or when they die, remove the old blossoms. This is called deadheading and can help you get flowers all summer long.

5 They should flower after about a month.

4 After about 5–12 days, the seeds will germinate, and leaves will appear soon afterward.

29

SUNFLOWERS

Sunflowers are a wonderful plant to grow in your garden because they attract bees and insects and add spectacular bursts of color. The seeds of the fully grown sunflower also make excellent bird food. Sunflowers can be grown in your garden or in pots in a sunny space and are best sown in April and May after the last frost, and once the temperature of the soil reaches 50°F/10°C.

YOU WILL NEED:

- Small plant pots
- Compost
- Sunflower seeds
- Garden stakes and string

SEASON	HARVEST	ENVIRONMENT
Spring & summer	2–3 months	Outdoors

HOW TO GROW:

1 Fill your pots with compost. Poke a small hole in the middle with your finger—it needs to be 1–1½ inches deep.

2 Drop a seed in each hole, cover it with compost, then water well. Continue to water them when the compost feels dry.

3 After 1–2 weeks, you should begin to see shoots. When the plants grow too big for the pots, you can transplant them into larger pots or plant them out in a sunny garden spot.

4 As they grow, you will need to support them with garden stakes. Tie the stalks loosely to the stakes so that they don't get damaged.